P9-DFZ-968

WHALES

BLUE WHALES

JOHN F. PREVOST

ABDO & Daughters

599.51
(1)

Published by Abdo & Daughters, 4940 Viking Drive, Suite 622, Edina, Minnesota 55435.

Library bound edition distributed by Rockbottom Books, Pentagon Tower, P.O. Box 36036, Minneapolis, Minnesota 55435.

Copyright © 1995 by Abdo Consulting Group, Inc., Pentagon Tower, P.O. Box 36036, Minneapolis, Minnesota 55435 USA. International copyrights reserved in all countries. No part of this book may be reproduced in any form without written permission from the publisher.

Printed in the United States.

Cover Photo credit: Peter Arnold, Inc.

Interior Photo credits: Peter Arnold, Inc.

Edited by Bob Italia

Library of Congress Cataloging-in-Publication Data

Prevost, John F.
   Blue whales / John F. Prevost.
      p.   cm. — (Whales)
Includes bibliographical references and index.
   ISBN 1-56239-475-4
1. Blue whale—Juvenile literature. [1. Blue whale. 2. Whales.] I. Title.
II. Series: Prevost, John F. Whales.
QL737.C424P74 1995
599.5'1—dc20   95-9676
                                                                    CIP
                                                                    AC

ABOUT THE AUTHOR
John Prevost is a marine biologist and diver who has been active in conservation and education issues for the past 18 years. Currently he is living inland and remains actively involved in freshwater and marine husbandry, conservation and education projects.

Contents

BLUE WHALES AND FAMILY

Blue whales are **mammals** that live in the sea. Like humans, they breathe air with lungs, are **warm-blooded**, and **nurse** their young with milk.

Blue whales are the largest animals that have ever lived on land or in water. Hunting killed off nearly all the blue whales. In 1965, laws were passed to protect blue whales. Since then, the number of blue whales has grown.

Other names for the blue whale are great whale, **baleen**, Sibbald's rorqual, and sulfurbottom. Cousins to the blue whale are the humpback whale, gray whale, minke whale and right whale.

Blue whales are the largest animals that have ever lived on land or in water.

SIZE, SHAPE AND COLOR

Blue whales are 75 to 85 feet (23 to 26 meters) long. Before the whaling industry hunted them, blue whales reached 110 feet (33.5 meters) long.

Blue whales have broad bodies. Their 2 **blowholes** are slightly raised above their head and like all whales they breathe air through their blowholes. The **flippers** are long and thin, but appear short on this huge whale.

The blue whale is a light blue-gray over most of its body that becomes spotted with age. Some blue whales

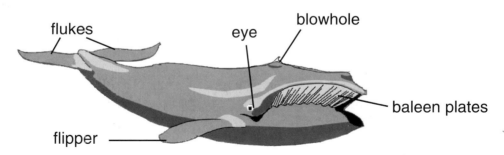

Baleen whales share the same features.

Blue whales have two blowholes that are raised above the head.

are marked with pale dots or stripes. The underside is a lighter blue or white.

On other blue whales, the belly turns yellow from tiny plants that grow on the skin. These blue whales are called sulfurbottoms. Blue whales are also called **baleen** whales because they have baleen plates instead of teeth.

WHERE THEY LIVE

Blue whales are found in oceans all around the world. They **migrate** from **polar** waters to **temperate** and **tropical** waters.

There are three large groups of blue whales: North Atlantic, North Pacific, and **Antarctic**. The **continents** and migration paths separate each group.

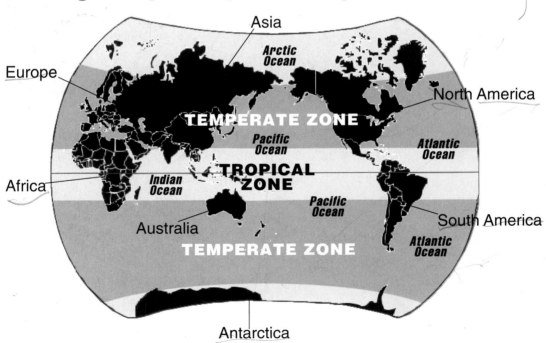

Blue whale watchers near Isla Donzante, Sea of Cortez, Mexico.

Blue whales travel from **feeding grounds** to **calving grounds**. They repeat the same paths year after year. A different blue whale type is found in the Indian Ocean. These blue whales do not **migrate**.

SENSES

Blue whales and people have 4 of the same senses. Their eyesight is good in and out of the water. If they are curious about activity above the water, blue whales can bob their heads above the water surface.

Hearing is their best sense. Because of its thickness, water passes on sound better than air.

Blue whales use **echolocation** to **communicate** with each other and to find food. To do this, blue whales make moans and clicks that travel long distances underwater. Touch and taste are also well developed. Blue whales do not have the sense of smell.

HOW ECHOLOCATION WORKS

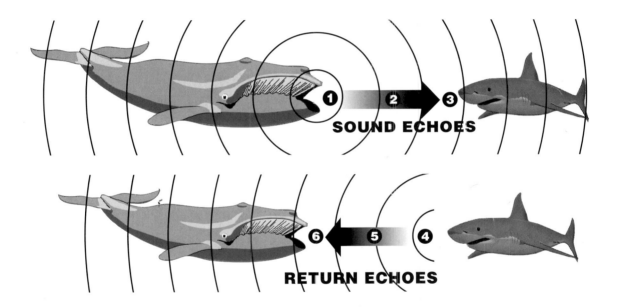

The whale sends out sound echoes (1). These echoes travel in all directions through the water (2). The sound echoes reach an object in the whale's path (3), then bounce off it (4). The return echoes travel through the water (5) and reach the whale (6). These echoes let the whale know where the object is, how large it is, and how fast it is moving.

DEFENSE

Killer whales will attack adult blue whales. Large sharks will attack calves and weak adults. Blue whales rely on their size and strength to fight off **predators**.

Man was the blue whale's leading predator. But now, hunting laws protect the blue whale.

Killer whales prey on the blue whale.

FOOD

Blue whales do not have any teeth. Instead they have 260 to 400 **baleen** plates attached on each side of the upper jaw. The plates bend and are lined with **bristles**.

A blue whale will fill its large throat with water and squeeze the water through the baleen with its tongue. The tiny food is trapped in the bristles. Blue whales have the longest baleen and the smallest straining bristles of all the whales.

Blue whales feed on small shellfish such as **copepods** and **krill**. The largest shellfish might measure only 2 inches (5 cm) long!

Scientists estimate that one blue whale eats 1.5 to 2 percent of its body weight daily. That's 4,500 to 6,000 pounds (2,040 to 2,720 kg) of krill for a 300,000-pound (136,000-kg) whale!

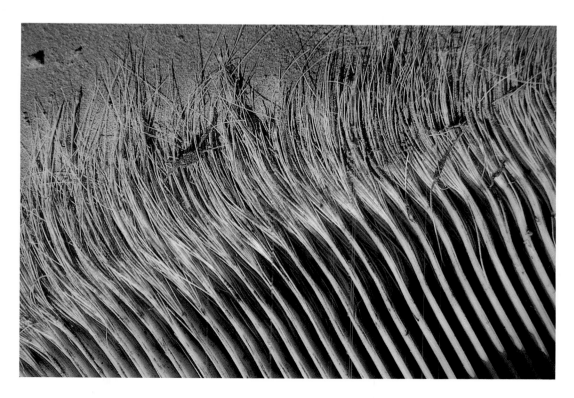

The baleen plates of a blue whale.

BABIES

A baby blue whale is called a **calf**. At birth, the calf is 20.5 to 24.5 feet (6.3 to 7.5 meters) long and blue-gray in color. Markings and spots develop as the whale grows older.

The blue whale calf needs its mother for the first year. Since whales are **mammals**, the calf will **nurse** for about 7 months. The young whale will not become an adult until it is 5 to 6 years old.

A blue whale and her calf in Baja California.

BLUE WHALE FACTS

Scientific Name
- Blue whale: *Balaenoptera musculus*
- Pygmy blue whale: *B. m. brevicauda*

Average Size
75 to 85 feet (23 to 26 meters) long

Where They're Found
All over the world in different groups:
- North Pacific group
- North Atlantic group
- Southern Hemisphere group
- Indian Ocean sub-species of pygmy blue whale

The huge tail fin of an adult blue whale.

GLOSSARY

ANTARCTIC - The south polar region.

BALEEN (buh-LEEN) - A hard flexible material growing in place of teeth and attached to the upper jaw; also called whalebone.

BLOWHOLE - A nostril (or nostrils) found on the top of the whale's head.

BRISTLE - A coarse, short, stiff hair.

CALF - A baby whale.

CALVING GROUNDS - An area where whales will go to safely bear their young.

COMMUNICATE (kuh-MEW-nih-kate) - To exchange or share feelings.

CONTINENT (KAHN-tih-nent) - One of the 7 main land masses: Europe, Asia, Africa, North America, South America, Australia and Antarctica.

COPEPODS (KOE-pih-pods) - Tiny shellfish representing over 7,500 species; and are an important food source for whales and fish.

ECOLOCATION (ek-oh-low-KAY-shun) - The use of sound waves to find objects.

FEEDING GROUNDS - An area where animals eat.

FLIPPERS - The forelimbs of a sea mammal.

KRILL - A group of shrimp-like shellfish representing 90 species, only found in open sea waters.

MAMMAL - A class of animals, including humans, that have hair and feed their young milk.

MIGRATION (my-GRAY-shun) - To travel periodically from one region to another in search of food or to reproduce.

NURSE - To feed a young animal or child milk from the mother's breast.

POLAR - Either the Arctic (north pole) or Antarctic (south pole) regions.

PREDATOR (PRED-uh-ter) - An animal that eats other animals.

PREY - Animals that are eaten by other animals.

SPECIES (SPEE-seas) - A group of related living things that have the same basic characteristics.

TEMPERATE (TEM-prit) - Moderate to cool water located between the polar and tropical waters.

TROPICAL (TRAH-pih-kull) - The part of the Earth near the equator where the oceans are very warm.

WARM-BLOODED - An animal whose body temperature remains the same and warmer than the outside air or water temperature.

Index

BIBLIOGRAPHY

Cousteau, Jacques-Yves. *The Whale, Mighty Monarch of the Sea.* N.Y.: Doubleday, 1972.

Dozier, Thomas A. *Whales and Other Sea Mammals.* Time-Life Films, 1977.

Leatherwood, Stephen. *The Sierra Club Handbook of Whales and Dolphins.* San Francisco, California: Sierra Club Books, 1983.

Minasian, Stanley M. *The World's Whales.* Washington, D.C.: Smithsonian Books, 1984.

Ridgway, Sam H., ed. *Mammals of the Sea.* Springfield, Illinois: Charles C. Thomas Publisher, 1972.